W9-DJI-593

BEYOND
CHICKEN

Project Editor: Lisa M. Tooker

Translator: Christie Tam

Editor: Lynda Zuber Sassi

Design & Typography: Elizabeth M. Watson

Photography & Recipes: Teubner Foodfoto Jmbh

Printed in China

ISBN: 1-59637-025-4

CONTENTS

THE BASICS

INTERNATIONAL FLAVORS

HEARTY . . . WITH VEGETABLES

DIVINE . . . WITH FRUIT

ON THE STOVETOP

INTRODUCTION

CHOOSE AN OCCASION and there's a perfect chicken meal to accompany it. Whether it's a chicken stew that warms the insides during the cold of winter, a chicken skewer grilled to perfection on the barbecue in summertime, or an exotic curry that satisfies your globetrotting craving for the evening. The versatile nature of chicken ensures that there is something for everyone.

THIS BOOK IS DIVIDED INTO FIVE SECTIONS. The chapter on Basics provides traditional classic recipes like Roasted Chicken as well as newer classics such as Chicken Wings. The chapter on International Flavors explores popular chicken dishes from around the world, focusing on ingredients specific to the country of origin. The chapters on vegetables and fruits pair chicken with the earthy, sweet, and tart flavors that come from Mother Nature. And, the chapter on preparing chicken on the stovetop provides a multitude of recipes that are quick, easy, and tasty.

We hope that this book will inspire you to revisit old favorites as well as add some new exotics to your chicken repertoire.

All recipes serve four.

CHICKEN FUNDAMENTALS

CHOOSING A CHICKEN

It goes without saying that the higher quality the chicken, the better results of the recipe. But, how to choose these days with so many options is the question. Most supermarkets offer a variety, which include store brand, name brand, free-range, and organic birds.

Name brand and store brand—there is little difference between these two except the packaging. Otherwise, they're probably grown side-by-side on the same farms. While they are inexpensive, they also have the least amount of flavor and tend to be soft. There are also the social and environmental issues to consider such as habitat, what they're fed, hormones, and drugs that they're given.

"Free-range" and organic are loosely defined terms. Generally speaking, what you're getting is a chicken that has been raised in less crowded conditions, has access to roam outside, has been fed an organic diet, and has not been treated with hormones or antibiotics. Reputable brands include Rocky, Bell and Evans, and Murray's.

Chicken is sold whole (fryers 2¾ to 4 pounds, and roasters 5 to 8 pounds), quartered, halved, or in assorted pieces. Chicken is available with skin or without, boneless or with bones, and frozen and fresh. Choose a chicken that looks plump and evenly colored. Be sure to check the sell-by date on the package. For maximum flexibility, buy the whole bird and cut it up yourself.

STORING CHICKEN
Refrigerate chicken immediately for up to 48 hours. Chicken can also be stored in the freezer in a zipper bag for up to six months. Defrost chicken in the refrigerator, not at room temperature to avoid harmful bacteria. If your chicken has an unpleasant odor, rinse it and pat dry. If after five minutes it still has an odor, then it is probably not good.

CHICKEN SAFETY
Chicken is highly perishable. It should not sit out in room temperature for more than one hour. Before and after handling raw chicken, wash your hands thoroughly with warm, soapy water. Wash all cutting surfaces, kitchen tools, and bowls that raw chicken comes into contact with. Finally, be sure that your chicken is thoroughly cooked to an internal temperature of 170° F.

CHECKING FOR DONENESS
Chicken needs to be cooked to a minimum temperature of 160° F to be sure that harmful bacteria such as salmonella are killed. To test for doneness, use a meat thermometer for certainty. To test a whole bird, insert the thermometer into the thickest part of the thigh, not touching any bones. It should register 170°F. To test a boneless piece, press the center. It should feel firm and spring back from your touch. To test a bone-in piece, make an incision near the bone. The meat should be opaque, with no sign of pink. While it's important not to undercook chicken, the same goes for over-cooking. Chicken that is over-cooked is dry and chewy.

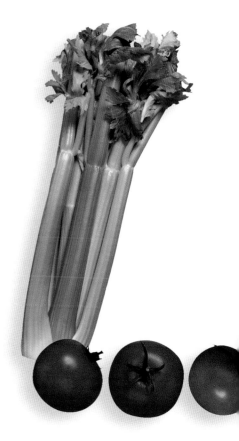

THE BASICS

CERTAIN CHICKEN DISHES are the staples from which many a meal has spawn. Our basics include traditional classics like Coq au Vin, the cornerstone for an elegant meal. Who doesn't like the feeling of comfort that comes with slurping the noodles in a bowl of Chicken Noodle Soup? Our basics wouldn't be complete without adding the modern classic, Chicken Wings. What could be better than cheering for the home team while licking the sauce from your fingers?

Coq au Vin

3½ lb assorted chicken pieces
2 tbs vegetable oil
2 oz smoked bacon, diced
¼ cup butter
1 clove garlic, chopped finely
⅔ cup onions, diced
½ cup carrots, diced finely
1 bottle red wine (e.g., Beaujolais)
2 bay leaves
1 bouquet garni (fresh parsley,
    marjoram, and thyme
    tied together)
3 tbs tomato paste
⅔ cup mushrooms, cleaned
    and cut in half
Kosher salt
Freshly ground pepper

PREHEAT OVEN TO 400°F.

RINSE CHICKEN and pat dry. Season with salt and pepper.

IN A CASSEROLE DISH, heat oil and brown bacon. Discard grease, add butter, and heat until foamy. Add chicken and brown on all sides. Add garlic, onions, and carrot. Cook for 10 minutes. Add wine, bay leaves, bouquet garni, and tomato paste. Cover and braise in preheated oven for 50 minutes, until chicken is tender. Remove from oven and add mushrooms. Return to oven and cook for 10 more minutes.

TO SERVE: Divide chicken onto plates and serve over rice. Drizzle with sauce.

Chicken Roasted
in White Wine

2 young whole chickens
½ cup olive oil
5 small onions, peeled
    and quartered
5 oz smoked ham, diced
1⅓ lb small potatoes, peeled
½ cup dry white wine
Kosher salt
Freshly ground pepper

PREHEAT OVEN TO 350°F.

RINSE CHICKEN and pat dry.
Rub interior and exterior with salt
and pepper, brush generously with
oil, and brown on all sides in a
large Dutch oven. Remove and
keep warm.

IN THE PAN RESIDUES, brown
onions, remove, and set aside. Add
ham and braise for 5 minutes. Add
chicken, onions, potatoes and wine,
and bake in the oven for about
20 minutes or until done.

SERVE with potatoes on the side.

Chicken Wings

3 dried bay leaves, crushed finely
½ tsp caraway seeds, ground
½ tsp coriander
½ tsp cumin
1 tsp yellow mustard powder
2 tsp Hungarian sweet paprika
1 tsp thyme, chopped finely
1 chile pepper, seeds removed
    and chopped finely
2 tbs lime juice
2 tbs brandy
2 tbs vegetable oil
12 chicken wings
Kosher salt

PREHEAT OVEN TO 375° F. Combine all ingredients except chicken in a food processor and process into a paste. Place wings on a baking sheet and brush on all sides with paste. Cover and marinate in the refrigerator for 30 minutes.

REMOVE WINGS from the refrigerator and bake in the preheated oven for 25–30 minutes.

SERVE wings with chili sauce, sweet-and-sour sauce, barbecue sauce, or salsa.

Chicken

Noodle Soup

4 cups water
⅔ cup leeks, white part only,
    sliced into matchsticks
1 small piece ginger, peeled
    and flattened
1 lb chicken breast fillets
3 tbs rice wine
10 oz dried wheat noodles
2 tbs butter
4 fresh shiitake mushrooms,
    cut into wide strips
⅔ cup canned bamboo shoots,
    cut into strips
⅔ cup bok choy, cut into strips
1 tbs soy sauce
Cilantro leaves for garnish
Kosher salt
Freshly ground pepper

IN A LARGE POT, combine 4 cups water, leeks, and ginger. Bring to a boil. Add chicken and bring to a boil. Reduce heat and simmer for 20 minutes, skimming off foam until the stock is clear. Remove chicken and let cool. Remove and discard chicken skin. Slice chicken into strips. Cover chicken and set aside.

ADD RICE WINE to the stock and simmer gently for 10 minutes. Strain the stock and set aside.

IN A SEPARATE POT, cook noodles in boiling, salted water according to package directions until barely soft.

HEAT BUTTER IN A PAN and briefly brown mushrooms and bamboo strips. Add bok choy and sauté for 30 seconds. Season to taste with salt and pepper. Add strained stock, soy sauce, chicken, and noodles. Bring to a gentle simmer then reduce heat.

TO SERVE: Place in warm bowls and garnish with individual cilantro leaves for color.

Chicken Stock

2½ lb assorted chicken pieces
1 carrot, chopped coarsely
1 celery stalk with leaves,
    chopped coarsely
1 leek, chopped coarsely
1 parsnip, chopped coarsely
1 onion, quartered
1 clove garlic, peeled
1 bunch Italian parsley
1 sprig thyme
Nutmeg
Kosher salt
Freshly ground pepper

RINSE CHICKEN and pat dry. In a large pot, place chicken and cover with 8 cups of water. Bring to a boil, reduce heat, and lightly simmer over low heat for 1 hour. Add carrot, celery, leek, parsnip, onion, garlic, parsley, and thyme. Simmer gently for about 30 minutes.

REMOVE CHICKEN to use in another dish. Pour stock through a fine-mesh strainer and into a clean pot. Remove fat from the hot stock, by placing a flat spoon on the surface so that as much fat and as little stock as possible runs into it. Or, refrigerate stock overnight and the fat will rise to the top where it is easily removed as a solid.

BEFORE SERVING, season stock with nutmeg, salt, and pepper.

MAKES ABOUT 2 QUARTS

TIP

► When making stock, you know the temperature is right when small bubbles rise very slowly and the surface is almost still.
► A boiled stewing chicken can easily be prepared as fried chicken.
► Or serve the chicken with a vinaigrette or horseradish cream as an appetizer on lettuce, or with bread for dinner.
► Stock is best if you use a fully grown, free-range chicken. Younger chickens yield a less aromatic stock.
► Feel free to add more vegetables to your stock for more flavor and variety.

INTERNATIONAL FLAVORS

POPULAR AROUND THE GLOBE, chicken has been interpreted in virtually all cultures. This section begins with a mild Swiss-Style Roast Chicken, made especially Swiss with the addition of Emmenthaler cheese, and ends in Latin America with a zingy Mexican Chicken Salad. Each recipe features ingredients that are unique to the country of origin.

Swiss-Style Roast Chicken

2¼ lb whole chicken
3 tbs vegetable oil
2 tbs butter
½ cup onions, diced
½ cup cooked ham, diced into
    small cubes
⅔ cup tomatoes, seeds removed
    and diced
½ tsp curry powder
¼ tsp Hungarian sweet paprika
⅔ cup chicken stock
¼ cup grated Emmenthaler cheese
1 tbs chopped parsley
Kosher salt
Freshly ground pepper

PREHEAT OVEN TO 425° F.
Rinse chicken interior and exterior
and pat dry. Combine oil, salt and
pepper, and brush onto chicken
interior and exterior. Place chicken
in a baking dish and bake for about
40 minutes.

IN A PAN, melt butter and sauté
onions and ham for 2–3 minutes.
Add tomatoes, curry, and paprika.
Stir and remove from heat.

REMOVE CHICKEN from the oven
and cut into 8 pieces. Set aside. Add
stock to pan juices and bring to a
boil. Reduce heat and skim fat off
the top. Add onion-ham mixture,
season with salt and pepper, and
return to a boil. Reduce heat and
return chicken to the pan, basting
with juices. Sprinkle with the
Emmenthaler and return to the
oven for 5 minutes. Garnish with
fresh parsley.

Greek Lemon Chicken

5 cloves garlic, peeled and minced
2 tbs kosher salt
¼ cup olive oil
Juice from 1 lemon
1 tsp chopped fresh oregano
3 tsp freshly ground pepper
2½ lb whole chicken
2 sprigs rosemary
1 lemon, cut into 8 pieces

IN A BOWL, combine garlic, salt, olive oil, lemon juice, oregano, and ground pepper.

RINSE CHICKEN interior and exterior and pat dry. Brush on all sides with garlic mixture. Place remaining marinade in chicken cavity with a sprig of rosemary and close the opening with toothpicks. Tie legs together, cover, and place in the refrigerator for 30 minutes.

PREHEAT OVEN TO 425° F. Place chicken in a baking dish and roast in the oven for 50 minutes. Strip needles from remaining rosemary sprig, chop, and sprinkle onto chicken 5 minutes before it's done roasting.

TO SERVE: Cut chicken into 4 pieces and garnish with lemon.

Portuguese Rice with Chicken

2 chicken breast fillets, butterflied
Juice from 1 orange
1 tsp lemon juice
1 shallot, peeled and chopped finely
1 tbs olive oil
⅓ cup butter, separated
1 small onion, chopped
½ clove garlic, minced
1 cup Arborio rice
¼ cup white wine
3 cups chicken stock
1 pinch saffron
8 black olives
Kosher salt
Freshly ground pepper

RINSE CHICKEN and pat dry. Season with salt and pepper. In a shallow bowl, combine orange juice, lemon juice, shallot, and olive oil. Add chicken and baste thoroughly. Cover, and place in the refrigerator for at least 12 hours to marinate.

PREHEAT OVEN TO 400° F. In an ovenproof pan, heat 3 tablespoons of butter. Remove chicken from marinade and brown. Place the pan in the oven for 20 minutes, brushing occasionally with marinade. Remove from oven, cover to keep warm, and set aside.

MAKE THE RISOTTO, in a pot, heat remaining butter. Add onion and garlic and braise 2–3 minutes—do not brown. Add rice and cook until translucent, then add wine, and reduce. Gradually add stock, stirring constantly. Add saffron and stir. Add more stock so the rice is covered. Simmer over moderate heat for 15–20 minutes, stirring frequently.

TO SERVE: Put rice into a shallow bowl, arrange chicken on top, and garnish with olives.

Tunisian Saffron Chicken

3½ lb assorted chicken pieces
3 tbs vegetable oil
1 onion, diced finely
¼ cup celery, diced
2 cloves garlic, minced
¼ tsp saffron threads
¼ tsp freshly grated ginger root
1 cup chicken stock
⅔ cup pumpkin or squash, cut
　　into matchsticks
½ cup small black olives
1 tsp chopped mint leaves
Kosher salt
Freshly ground pepper

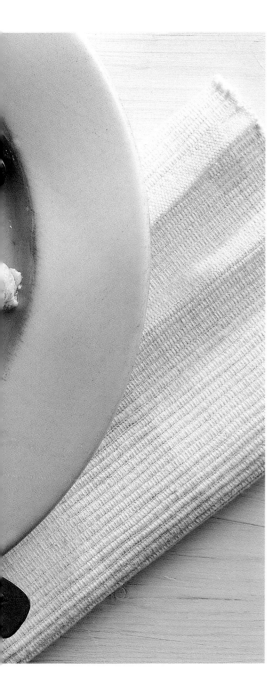

RINSE CHICKEN and pat dry. Season with salt and pepper.

IN A PAN, heat oil and brown chicken on all sides. Add onions, celery and garlic, and sauté for 5–7 minutes. Add saffron, ginger, and season with salt and pepper. Add stock and braise over low heat for 25–30 minutes. Add pumpkin and olives and braise for 5 minutes. Season to taste with salt and pepper and serve with mint leaves.

Mauritian Chicken and Shrimp Curry

1½ cups basmati rice
½ cup (1 stick) butter, separated
½ lb chicken breast fillets
½ lb shrimp, peeled and deveined
¼ cup peanut oil
½ tbs minced fresh ginger
2 cloves garlic, minced
1 green chile pepper, seeds
    removed and diced finely
½ cup onions, chopped finely
1 tsp turmeric
2 tsp mild curry powder
⅔ lb tomatoes, diced
1¼ cups water
1 tbs cilantro, chopped finely
¼ cup green onions, chopped finely
Kosher salt
Freshly ground pepper

PREHEAT OVEN TO 350° F. Rinse rice under cold water. In a saucepan, bring 2 cups water to a boil. Add salt and 2 tablespoons butter. Add rice and boil for 10 minutes or until done. Drain. In a baking dish, melt ¼ cup butter and add rice. Using a spoon, form 4 wells in the rice that are 2 inches from the edges. Cut remaining butter into 4 pieces and place one piece in each well. Cover and bake for 30 minutes. When the surface is golden and crispy, the rice is done.

RINSE CHICKEN and shrimp and pat dry. Cut chicken into 1 inch pieces. Season chicken and shrimp with salt and pepper.

IN A LARGE PAN, heat oil, sauté shrimp for 2–3 minutes and remove. In the same pan, brown chicken and remove. Add ginger, garlic, chile pepper and onions, and brown for 2 minutes, stirring constantly. Add turmeric and curry powder and brown over medium heat for 2 minutes while stirring. Add tomatoes and simmer for 2–3 minutes. Return chicken and shrimp to the pan, add water, and simmer for 10 minutes. Add cilantro and green onions and simmer for 2–3 minutes. Season to taste with salt and pepper.

TO SERVE: Scoop rice into bowls and serve with the curry over the top.

Tandoori Chicken

2 lb chicken breast and thigh fillets
Juice from 1 lime
1 tsp salt
½ tsp black pepper
1 cup plain yogurt
¼ cup wine vinegar
2 tbs peanut oil
¼ cup onion, chopped
2 cloves garlic, minced
1 tbs minced ginger root
2 tsp coriander
2 tsp cumin
¼ tsp turmeric
2 tsp Hungarian sweet paprika
½ tsp chili powder

RINSE CHICKEN and pat dry. Score skin, rub with lime juice, salt, and pepper. Let stand for 30 minutes.

IN A BOWL, combine yogurt, vinegar, and oil. Mix thoroughly. Add onion, garlic, ginger, coriander, cumin, turmeric, paprika, and chili powder. Process into a paste. Place chicken in a baking dish and rub thoroughly with seasoning. Cover dish with aluminum foil and refrigerate overnight.

REMOVE CHICKEN 1 hour before roasting, and rub again with seasoning. Preheat oven to 400° F. Place chicken in a roasting pan and cover with foil. Bake for 20 minutes, remove foil, and bake for 10 more minutes.

Riz Yollof

1⅓ lb chicken breast fillets
2 tsp Hungarian sweet paprika
3 tbs peanut oil
½ cup onions, peeled and chopped
3 cloves garlic, peeled and minced
2 chile peppers, halved and
    seeds removed
1 cinnamon stick
½ tsp allspice
1 tsp turmeric
1 cup long-grain rice
1½ cups chicken stock
3/4 cup tomato juice
½ cup carrots, peeled and cut
    into matchsticks
½ lb cooked ham, cut into cubes
1 cup tomatoes, chopped
½ cup frozen peas
Kosher salt
Freshly ground pepper

CUT CHICKEN into 1 inch pieces and season with paprika, salt, and pepper. In a large sauce pan, over medium heat, add oil and brown chicken on all sides. Add onions, garlic, chile peppers, cinnamon, allspice, turmeric, and rice. Add stock and tomato juice and season with salt and pepper. Bring to a boil, reduce heat, cover, and simmer gently for 10 minutes. Add carrots and ham and simmer for another 10 minutes. Add tomatoes and peas, and simmer for 5–8 minutes, adding more stock if necessary, and stirring occasionally.

SEASON TO TASTE with salt and ground pepper.

Indian Coconut Chicken

1 crushed dried chile pepper
1 tsp crushed coriander seeds
½ tsp crushed black peppercorns
1 tsp crushed cumin seeds
1 tsp turmeric
¼ cup peanut oil
½ cup onions, peeled and
    diced finely
3 cloves garlic, peeled and minced
1 tbs fresh ginger root, peeled
    and minced
1 green chile pepper, seeds removed
    and diced finely
1⅔ lb chicken breast fillets, cubed
¾ cup chicken stock
1½ cups coconut milk
1 tsp lime juice
1 tbs finely chopped cilantro
    for garnish
Kosher salt

IN AN UNGREASED PAN, roast chile pepper, coriander, peppercorns, cumin, and turmeric until they give off an aroma (1–2 minutes); set aside.

IN A PAN, heat oil and sauté onions for 3–4 minutes. Add garlic, ginger, chile pepper, and chicken. Sauté for 8–10 minutes while stirring. Add set aside roasted spices, chicken stock, and coconut milk. Simmer gently for about 20 minutes. Season to taste with lime juice and salt.

SERVE over basmati rice and garnish with cilantro.

Thai Curry Chicken

2 green chile peppers, seeds
    removed and diced finely
1 tbs cilantro, chopped finely
½ tsp lemon grass, diced finely
1 tsp fresh ginger root, peeled
    and diced
1 tsp fresh galangal root, peeled
    and diced
1 fresh kaffir lime leaf, cut
    into strips
¼ cup green onions, peeled and
    diced finely
2 cloves garlic, peeled and
    diced finely
½ tsp crushed coriander seeds
½ tsp crushed cumin seeds
3 lb chicken breast and thigh fillets
3 tbs peanut oil
¼ cup chicken stock
2 cups coconut milk
¾ cup red bell peppers, seeds
    removed and diced
⅓ cup snow peas, ends trimmed
    and cut in half
Juice from ½ lime
Thai basil leaves for garnish
Kosher salt
Freshly ground pepper

COMBINE chile peppers, cilantro, lemon grass, ginger, galangal, kaffir leaf, onions, garlic, coriander and cumin seeds, and process in a blender to make a fine paste. Set aside.

RINSE CHICKEN and pat dry. Cut into 1 inch pieces. In a large pan, heat oil and sauté chicken in batches for 2–3 minutes until golden-brown, stirring occasionally. Return all chicken to the pan, add set aside curry paste, and stir-fry for 1 minute. Add stock, briefly bring to a boil, and season with salt. Add half the coconut milk, cover, and simmer gently for 5 minutes. Add remaining coconut milk, bell peppers, and snow peas. Simmer uncovered for 8–12 minutes. Add lime juice and season to taste with salt and pepper.

SERVE garnished with basil leaves on top of jasmine rice.

Vietnamese Peppered Chicken Skewers

1¾ lb chicken breast fillets
1 tbs black peppercorns
½ tbs coarse sea salt
¼ cup apricot marmalade
4 cloves garlic, peeled and minced
2 tbs fish sauce
Zest from 1 lime
Juice from 1–2 limes
Several iceberg lettuce leaves
¾ cup diced cucumber
5 oz cooked rice noodles
Several fresh mint leaves
    for garnish

Wooden skewers, soaked in water

PREHEAT OVEN TO 400° F. Rinse chicken and pat dry. Cut chicken into 1 inch cubes.

IN AN UNGREASED PAN, roast peppercorns until they give off an aroma (be careful not to burn). Crush finely in a mortar and transfer to a shallow bowl. Add salt, marmalade, garlic, fish sauce, lime zest, and lime juice. Mix well. Marinate meat in mixture for 30 minutes, then thread onto skewers. Arrange skewers on a baking sheet and cook in the preheated oven for 4–5 minutes on each side.

TO SERVE: Divide skewers on top of lettuce leaves. Serve noodles on the side. Top with cucumbers and garnish with mint leaves.

Tea-Smoked Chicken

Marinade

3 tbs peanut oil

⅔ cup fresh ginger root, peeled and chopped finely

1½ tbs vodka

2 tsp Chinese five-spice powder

1 tsp coarse sea salt

1 tbs chili oil

4 chicken breast fillets

¼ cup sugar

¼ cup flour

¼ cup green tea leaves

5 star anise

2 cinnamon sticks (fried)

MAKE THE MARINADE: Combine oil, ginger, vodka, five-spice powder, salt, and chili oil in a shallow bowl. Score chicken breasts 3–4 times diagonally. Place chicken in the marinade and brush on all sides. Cover and marinate overnight in the refrigerator.

THE NEXT DAY, prepare the smoking ingredients. Combine sugar, flour, tea leaves, star anise, and cinnamon in a bowl. Line a wok with aluminum foil. Distribute smoking mixture on top. Place a round filter or steamer in the wok. Put chicken in the filter and cover securely around the edges with a piece of aluminum foil. Carefully pierce foil several times. Cover the wok with a lid and turn heat to medium-high. Smoke for 15 minutes, turn off the wok, and let stand for another 5–10 minutes.

TO SERVE: Slice chicken crosswise, and arrange on a platter over sticky rice or glass noodles. Use plum, chili, soy, or hoisin sauce as condiments.

Laotian Chicken Salad

½ lb chicken breast and thigh fillets
3 green onions, chopped in thirds
2 celery stalks, chopped coarsely
1 tbs ginger root, sliced
2 carrots, chopped coarsely

Dressing
1 tbs dark brown sugar
1 tbs rice vinegar
Juice from 1 kaffir lime
3 tbs fish sauce
1 red chile pepper, seeds removed
    and cut into rings
2 cloves garlic, peeled and minced
3 tbs peanut oil

Salad
1 head of white cabbage,
    sliced thinly
⅓ cup white onions, sliced thinly
½ cup carrots, sliced into
    thin matchsticks
¼ cup mint leaves, cut into strips

RINSE CHICKEN AND PAT DRY. In a large pot, combine 4 cups water, green onions, celery, ginger and carrots, and bring to a boil. Add chicken and salt lightly. Add additional water if necessary to cover the chicken. Reduce heat and simmer for 30 minutes. Remove chicken and cool.

MAKE THE DRESSING: In a bowl, combine brown sugar, vinegar, lime juice, and fish sauce. Whisk together until sugar dissolves. Stir in chile pepper, garlic, and oil. Season with salt and pepper to taste.

MAKE THE SALAD: In a bowl, toss cabbage, onions, carrots, and chicken with the dressing and mint leaves. Let stand for 10 minutes then serve garnished with cilantro.

TIP

▶ Cilantro has a lively, pungent fragrance and distinct flavor. It can be used fresh or dry.
▶ Cilantro is the most commonly utilized herb in the world, spanning the globe from Asia to Latin America to the Caribbean.

Mexican

Chicken Salad

⅔ lb chicken breast fillets

1 tbs olive oil

1 red bell pepper, seeds removed
and cut into strips

1 green bell pepper, seeds removed
and cut into strips

1 can (15 oz) corn, drained

1 can (15 oz) pineapple
rings, cubed

1 cup frozen peas, cooked

Dressing

⅔ cup reduced fat mayonnaise

1 container (6 oz) sour cream

2 tbs lemon juice

½ tsp curry powder

Pinch of sugar

Kosher salt

Freshly ground pepper

RINSE CHICKEN, pat dry, and season with salt and pepper. Heat oil in a pan and brown chicken on each side. Reduce heat to low and cook for 10 minutes. Remove, cool for 5 minutes, and cut into cubes.

IN A BOWL, combine bell peppers, corn, pineapple, peas, and chicken.

MAKE THE DRESSING: In a small bowl, combine mayonnaise, sour cream, lemon juice, and curry. Season to taste with sugar, salt, and pepper.

TO SERVE: Pour dressing over salad, toss gently, and divide onto plates.

Sicilian Roast Chicken

3 lb assorted chicken pieces
4 cloves garlic, minced
1 tsp coarse sea salt
¼ cup softened butter
1 red pepperoncini, seeds removed
    and chopped finely
⅓ cup plus 1 tbs olive oil, separated

Marinade
¼ cup lemon juice
¾ cup orange juice
2 tbs lemon liqueur
    (e.g., Limoncello)
1 tbs parsley, chopped finely
Zest from 1 orange

PREHEAT OVEN TO 375° F. Rinse chicken and pat dry. In a bowl, combine garlic, sea salt, butter, and pepperoncini. Rub thoroughly into chicken.

IN A ROASTING PAN, heat 1 tablespoon olive oil and briefly brown chicken. Place pan in the oven and roast for 40–45 minutes, basting occasionally with juices.

IN A LARGE, DEEP BOWL, combine lemon juice, orange juice, remaining olive oil, lemon liqueur, parsley, and orange zest. Add hot chicken and cover thoroughly with marinade.

TO SERVE: Divide chicken onto plates and drizzle with additional marinade from the bowl.

HEARTY. . . WITH VEGETABLES

THERE'S NEVER A VEGETABLE that doesn't partner well with chicken—turnips in winter; sweet asparagus in spring; ripe, juicy tomatoes in the summer. Stir-fried, roasted side-by-side, or strung on a skewer, the combination of chicken and vegetables will warm the insides and satisfy the soul.

Steamed Chicken and Vegetables

½ cup kohlrabi, peeled and cut
   into matchsticks
½ cup carrots, peeled and cut
   into matchsticks
⅓ cup snow peas, ends trimmed
   and cut into strips
½ cup spinach, cleaned and cut
   into strips
¼ cup green onions, cut into pieces
1⅓ lb chicken breast fillet, sliced
1 tsp peanut oil
3 tbs sesame seeds
1½ cups chicken stock

Vinaigrette
2 tbs fish sauce
1 tbs lime juice
1 tbs rice vinegar
2 tbs sesame oil
Several fresh mint leaves
   for garnish
Kosher salt
Freshly ground pepper

COMBINE kohlrabi, carrots, snow peas, spinach, and onions in a steamer. Place chicken on top of vegetables and season with salt and pepper.

IN A PAN, heat peanut oil, add sesame seeds, roast seeds until golden, remove, and let cool.

IN A SAUCEPAN, bring stock to a boil. Insert steamer, cover, and steam for 8–10 minutes.

FOR THE VINAIGRETTE: Combine fish sauce, lime juice, vinegar, and oil. Add ⅓ cup of the steaming stock liquid. Mix together.

TO SERVE: Divide chicken and vegetables onto plates, drizzle with vinaigrette, and sprinkle with sesame seeds. Garnish with mint leaves. Use remaining vinaigrette as a dip on the side.

Chicken with Sweet Asparagus

Stuffing

4 boneless chicken thighs
⅓ cup heavy cream
1 chile pepper, seeds removed and
    diced finely
2 tbs candied ginger, diced
Pinch of turmeric
4 chicken breast fillets with skin

Asparagus

12 spears white asparagus, peeled
1 lemon, sliced
Pinch of sugar
3 tbs butter, separated
½ cup red bell pepper, diced

Sauce

1 cup chicken stock
2 tsp ginger syrup
1 tsp molasses
1½ tbs balsamic vinegar

Shoestring potatoes

½ lb firm potatoes, peeled and
    cut into thin matchsticks
Vegetable oil
Kosher salt
Freshly ground pepper

RINSE CHICKEN and pat dry. Season with salt and pepper.

MAKE THE STUFFING: Chop chicken thighs coarsely and combine with cream. Purée in a blender. Add chile, ginger, and turmeric. Season to taste with salt and pepper. Cut a pocket in each chicken breast, fill with stuffing, close, and refrigerate.

MAKE THE ASPARAGUS: Place 1 lemon slice, sugar, and 1 tablespoon of butter in a pot containing a large amount of salted water and bring to a boil. Add asparagus and cook for 8–10 minutes. Remove and drain. Cut asparagus in half lengthwise and then cut into uniform pieces. In a pan, heat butter and brown asparagus. Add bell peppers and sauté briefly.

MAKE THE SAUCE: Reduce stock by half. Add ginger syrup, molasses, and balsamic vinegar. Season to taste with salt and pepper. Set aside.

PREHEAT THE OVEN TO 350° F. Remove chicken from the refrigerator. In a hot pan, brown chicken in remaining 2 tablespoons butter. Finish cooking in the preheated oven for 10 minutes.

MAKE THE SHOESTRING POTATOES: In a large pan, heat oil to 350°F and deep-fry potatoes in batches. Remove, drain, and salt lightly.

TO SERVE: Arrange asparagus in the center of each plate, top with chicken, and drizzle with sauce. Serve shoestring potatoes on the side.

Stir-Fried Chicken with Vegetables

1 lb assorted chicken breast and
 thigh fillets
¼ cup peanut oil, separated
⅓ cup green beans, ends trimmed
 and cut into pieces
3 tbs green onions, chopped into
 fine rings
1 clove garlic, peeled and minced
2 tsp fresh ginger root, peeled
 and minced
1 chile pepper, seeds removed and
 cut into fine rings
½ cup zucchini, cut into cubes
½ cup green bell peppers, seeds
 removed and cut into strips
⅓ cup carrots, peeled and
 sliced finely
½ cup chopped tomatoes, seeds
 removed and cut into cubes
¾ cup chicken stock
¼ cup light soy sauce
1 tbs oyster sauce
½ tsp cornstarch
Cilantro
¼ cup pumpkin seeds, toasted
Kosher salt
Freshly ground pepper

PREHEAT OVEN TO 325° F. Rinse chicken and pat dry. Season with salt and pepper. In an oven-proof pan, heat 2 tablespoons of oil. Add chicken and brown on all sides. Bake in preheated oven for 30–40 minutes.

IN A POT, blanch green beans in salted water for 2–3 minutes, rinse under cold water, and drain. Set aside.

IN A WOK, heat remaining oil and briefly brown onions, garlic, ginger, and chile pepper. Add zucchini, bell peppers, carrots and set aside green beans, and cook for 6–8 minutes, stirring occasionally. Add tomatoes.

IN A BOWL, combine stock, soy sauce, oyster sauce and cornstarch, and pour into wok and bring to a boil. Slice chicken and add to wok. Stir everything together and season to taste with salt and pepper.

TO SERVE: Sprinkle with cilantro and pumpkin seeds.

Chicken and Vegetable Curry

1 lb chicken breast fillets
1 red chile pepper, seeds removed
    and diced
1 tbs fresh ginger root, minced
1 clove garlic, minced
1 tbs cilantro, chopped finely
1 tbs mild curry powder
⅓ cup peanut oil, separated
½ cup snow peas, ends trimmed
    and cut into pieces
¼ cup green onions, cut into rings
1 cup red bell peppers, seeds
    removed and cubed
¾ cup small canned mushrooms,
    drained
¾ cup pineapple (canned or fresh),
    cut into pieces
1¼ cups coconut milk
2 tbs peanut oil
Kosher salt
Freshly ground pepper

CUT CHICKEN BREAST into ½ inch strips, and season with salt and pepper. In a bowl, combine chile pepper, ginger, garlic, cilantro, curry powder, and ¼ cup oil. Add chicken, and coat thoroughly with curry mixture. Cover, and marinate in the refrigerator for 30 minutes.

IN A PAN, heat remaining oil and fry chicken in batches over medium heat for 2–3 minutes, then remove. Add snow peas, onions and bell peppers, and brown briefly. Add mushrooms, pineapple and chicken, pour in coconut milk, and simmer for 10 minutes. Season to taste with salt and pepper and serve over Chinese egg noodles or rice.

Braised Chicken
with Turnips

4 chicken legs and thighs
1 tbs Hungarian sweet paprika
2 tbs olive oil
⅓ cup carrots, peeled and
    cut into matchsticks
⅔ cup small white turnips, peeled
    and cut into matchsticks
1 cup small firm potatoes
⅓ cup white onions, peeled and
    cut into rings
1 clove garlic, diced
¾ cup chicken stock
1 tbs lemon juice
Zest from ½ lemon
1 tbs parsley, chopped finely
Kosher salt
Freshly ground pepper

PREHEAT OVEN TO 350° F. Rinse chicken and pat dry. Season with salt, pepper, and paprika.

IN A ROASTING PAN, heat oil and brown chicken pieces on all sides. Remove chicken and set aside. Add carrots, turnips, potatoes, onions, and garlic to the roasting pan, season with salt and pepper. Add stock. Simmer for 5 minutes. Add chicken, lemon juice, and lemon zest. Cover and braise in the preheated oven on the middle rack for 20 minutes, occasionally basting with the stock. Remove cover and cook for another 10 minutes.

TO SERVE: Divide evenly onto plates, drizzle with pan juices, and sprinkle with parsley.

Braised Whole Chicken

1– 3 lb whole roasting chicken
½ tsp ginger
1 bouquet garni (fresh parsley,
    marjoram, and thyme
    tied together)
¼ cup butter
1 cup zucchini, sliced
1 lb small firm potatoes, peeled
    and sliced (if necessary)
½ cup corn
⅔ cup tomatoes, diced
2 cups chicken stock
1 bunch parsley, chopped finely
2 sprigs thyme, leaves removed
    and chopped finely
Kosher salt
Freshly ground pepper

PREHEAT OVEN TO 425° F. Rinse chicken and pat dry. Season interior and exterior with ginger, salt, and pepper. Place bouquet garni in the cavity. Truss chicken, separate the skin from the flesh, and rub the flesh with butter. Place in a roasting pan and brown in the oven for 10 minutes.

REMOVE CHICKEN from the oven, and add zucchini, potatoes, corn, and tomatoes around the sides of the pan. Add stock and reduce oven temperature to 350°F. Cook chicken for 20 minutes, basting occasionally with stock and pan juices.

SPRINKLE PARSLEY and thyme on chicken and cook for 30–40 more minutes, until done.

TO SERVE: Cut chicken into pieces and arrange on a platter surrounded by vegetables. Pour pan juices over the top.

Drumsticks in Vegetable Sauce

12 chicken legs
3 tbs olive oil
⅓ cup onions, diced finely
4 cloves garlic, minced
⅓ cup celery, sliced finely
⅔ cup red bell peppers, diced
⅔ cup green bell peppers, diced
⅓ cup carrots, sliced thinly
1 tbs oregano, chopped finely
1 tbs thyme, chopped finely
2 cups tomatoes, diced
½ cup white wine
½ cup chicken stock
¼ cup black olives
1 tbs chopped parsley
Kosher salt
Freshly ground pepper

PREHEAT OVEN TO 350° F. Rinse chicken and pat dry. Season with salt and pepper.

IN AN OVEN-PROOF PAN, heat oil and brown chicken on all sides. Remove chicken from pan. Reduce heat, add onions and garlic, and sauté. Add celery, bell peppers, carrots herbs, tomatoes, chicken, white wine, and stock. Season to taste with salt and pepper. Add olives, and place pan in preheated oven for 20–25 minutes, adding a little stock if necessary.

TO SERVE: Divide chicken evenly on plates, drizzle with pan juices, and sprinkle with parsley.

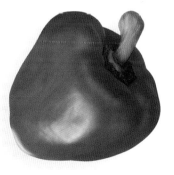

Chicken Stew with Summer Vegetables

2¼ lb chicken breast and
    thigh fillets
Pinch of Hungarian sweet paprika
2 tbs vegetable oil
⅓ cup onions, peeled and cut
    into rings
1 clove garlic, minced
2 tbs tomato paste
⅓ cup white wine
1½ cups chicken stock
½ cup carrots, peeled and cut
    into matchsticks
⅓ cup celery, sliced
½ cup cauliflower florets
½ cup zucchini, cubed
⅔ cup tomatoes, diced
1 cup peas
1 tsp thyme leaves
1 tbs chopped parsley
Kosher salt
Freshly ground pepper

RINSE CHICKEN and pat dry. Rub with salt, pepper, and paprika.

IN A LARGE POT, heat oil and brown chicken on all sides. Remove chicken and set aside.

IN THE SAME POT, add onions and garlic and braise until translucent. Stir in tomato paste and braise briefly. Add wine and reduce slightly. Add stock and bring to a boil. Reduce heat to simmer. Add chicken, carrots, and celery. Simmer for 10 minutes. Add cauliflower and simmer for 5 minutes. Add zucchini and tomatoes and simmer for 10 minutes. Add peas. Season to taste with salt, pepper, thyme, and parsley.

Chicken and Oyster Mushroom Salad

1¾ lb leeks, white part only, sliced into rings
14 oz oyster mushrooms
2 lb assorted boneless chicken pieces
⅓ cup plus 3 tbs vegetable oil, separated

Dressing
3 tbs white wine vinegar
Juice from ½ lemon
Pinch of sugar

1 cup red bell peppers, seeds removed and diced
⅓ cup white onions, peeled and chopped
1 tbs chopped chives
Kosher salt
Freshly ground pepper

BLANCH LEEKS in boiling salted water for 2 minutes, remove, and place in ice water. Separate oyster mushrooms from one another, remove stems, and cut caps into strips about ½ inch wide.

RINSE CHICKEN, pat dry, and season with salt and pepper. Cut chicken into 1 inch cubes.

IN A PAN, heat 2 tablespoons oil, and brown chicken for 3–4 minutes. Season with salt and pepper, remove, and let cool. Add 1 tablespoon oil to the pan, heat, and sauté mushrooms for 4 minutes. Season with salt and pepper, remove, and cool.

FOR THE DRESSING: Combine vinegar and lemon juice. Add remaining oil and season to taste with sugar, salt, and pepper. Whisk dressing together until creamy.

IN A BOWL, combine well-drained leeks, chicken, mushrooms, bell peppers, and onions. Add dressing and toss carefully. Sprinkle chives over the top.

DIVINE . . . WITH FRUIT

COMBINING SAVORY CHICKEN with sweet or tart fruit creates a flavor sensation for the taste buds. This section features the classic combination of Lemon Chicken and Thyme and the not so classic, Chicken with Papaya Guacamole. Serve these recipes to company, and they'll be talking about the meal for days.

Chicken Curry
with Apples

1 small yellow onion, peeled
    and diced
2 tbs butter
1 tbs curry powder
Juice from 1 orange
1 apple, peeled and cut into
    thin wedges
¼ cup heavy cream
⅔ lb chicken breast fillets
1 scallion, chopped into rings
Kosher salt
Freshly ground pepper

PREPARE IN THE MICROWAVE. Place onion and butter in a casserole dish. Cover, and braise on high until translucent, stirring once halfway through. Add curry and orange juice. Stir. Cover and cook for 4 minutes on high. Add apple, cream, and chicken. Cover, and cook on medium for 4 minutes. Season to taste with salt and pepper. Garnish with scallion rings.

FOR A VARIATION: Use turkey breast and pineapple.

Fried Chicken with Apple Chutney

Chutney

3 cups apples, peeled and diced

1 cup onions, peeled and diced

⅔ cup raisins

⅔ cup light brown sugar

¾ cup apple cider vinegar

1 tsp panch phoran (Indian
    5-spice blend)

2 tsp fresh ginger root, diced finely

1 red chile pepper, seeds removed
    and cut into fine strips

4 chicken breast fillets

1 tbs vegetable oil

2 tbs butter

⅔ cup chicken stock

Kosher salt

Freshly ground pepper

MAKE THE CHUTNEY: In a saucepan, combine apples, onions, raisins, sugar, vinegar, panch phoran, ginger, and chile pepper. Season lightly with salt and pepper and simmer over low heat for 45 minutes, stirring occasionally until the apples are tender. Remove from heat and cool.

RINSE CHICKEN and pat dry. Season with salt and pepper.

IN A PAN, heat oil and butter. Place chicken in the pan with the skin side down and fry over reduced heat for 12–15 minutes, turning occasionally. Remove chicken from the pan and set aside. Add stock to the same pan, season with salt and pepper, and reduce stock by half.

TO SERVE: Divide chicken onto plates and top with pan juices and the chutney.

Chicken with
Papaya Guacamole

½ cup light soy sauce

2 tbs Worcestershire sauce

¼ cup vegetable oil

1 tbs wasabi powder

½ cup fresh-squeezed orange juice

1½ tbs ginger root, grated finely

1½ tbs floral honey

½ tsp black pepper

3 lb boneless chicken pieces

Papaya guacamole

1¾ cups ripe papayas, peeled
    and diced

2 tbs shallots, chopped finely

½ cup tomatoes, seeds removed
    and diced

Juice from 1 lime

2 green chile peppers, seeds
    removed and chopped finely

1 tsp chopped cilantro

Kosher salt

Freshly ground pepper

Wooden skewers, soaked in water

IN A BOWL, combine soy sauce, Worcestershire sauce, vegetable oil, wasabi powder, orange juice, ginger, honey, and pepper. Stir until the honey is dissolved.

RINSE CHICKEN and pat dry. Season with salt and pepper and cut into 1½ inch cubes. Combine with marinade until chicken is coated on all sides. Allow chicken to marinate in the refrigerator 3–4 hours.

MAKE THE PAPAYA GUACAMOLE: Combine papayas, shallots, tomatoes, lime juice, salt, and pepper. Add chile peppers and cilantro.

REMOVE CHICKEN from refrigerator and thread onto skewers. Grill on a preheated barbecue 4–5 minutes on each side, occasionally brushing with the marinade.

TO SERVE: Arrange skewers on a serving dish with papaya guacamole on the side for dipping.

Barbecued Chicken with Spicy Mango Sauce

4 chicken breast fillets
3 tbs green onions, chopped into
    fine rings
1 clove garlic, minced
2 red chile pepper, seeds removed
    and diced finely
1 tbs parsley, chopped finely
¼ cup vegetable oil

Mango sauce
1⅓ cups mango, separated
    and cubed
⅓ cup coconut milk
⅔ cup chicken stock

⅓ cup cherry tomatoes, cut in half
Seeds from ½ pomegranate
Kosher salt
Freshly ground pepper

RINSE CHICKEN and pat dry. Season with salt and pepper. In a shallow bowl, combine onions, garlic, 1 chile pepper, parsley, and oil. Add chicken and baste thoroughly with the mixture. Cover and marinate in the refrigerator for 30 minutes.

FOR THE MANGO SAUCE: Purée ⅔ cup mango and put through a fine strainer. In a saucepan, combine mango, coconut milk, stock, and remaining chile pepper. Simmer for 10 minutes. Season to taste with salt and pepper.

REMOVE CHICKEN from marinade. Place on a preheated barbecue for 5 minutes on each side, brushing occasionally with marinade.

IN A PAN, briefly sauté remaining mango and tomatoes in a little oil and season with salt and pepper.

TO SERVE: Slice chicken and arrange on plates with mango, tomatoes, pomegranate seeds, and mango sauce.

Lemon Chicken
with Thyme

2½ lb assorted chicken pieces
3 tbs sunflower oil
½ cup pearl onions, peeled
½ cup red bell peppers, seeds
    removed and cut into fine strips
3 cloves garlic, peeled and diced
½ cup white wine
½ cup chicken stock
4 sprigs lemon thyme
Zest from 1 lemon
1 lemon, cut in half, separated
1 tbs thyme honey
Kosher salt
Freshly ground pepper

RINSE CHICKEN and pat dry. Season with salt and pepper.

PREHEAT OVEN TO 350° F. In a pan, heat oil and brown chicken until golden, starting with the skin sides. Remove, place in a baking dish, and set aside. In the same pan, brown onions, peppers, and garlic. Add wine and stock, bring to a boil, and pour over the chicken. Sprinkle chicken with lemon thyme and lemon zest. Place half the lemon on top of the chicken. Bake chicken in the preheated oven for 25 minutes.

IN A SMALL BOWL, squeeze juice from the other lemon half, combine with honey, and set aside. During the last 10 minutes of baking, brush chicken with honey-lemon sauce.

TO SERVE: Divide chicken onto plates and drizzle with pan juices.

Barbecued Chicken with Orange Marinade

4 lb assorted chicken pieces
4 cloves garlic, minced
1 tsp coarse sea salt
¾ cup olive oil, separated
1 tsp Tabasco sauce

Marinade
Juice from 2 lemons
Juice from 2 oranges
Zest from 2 oranges
2 tbs lemon liqueur
    (e.g., Limoncello)
3 tbs barbecue sauce
½ cup black olives, chopped
⅔ cup tomatoes, diced
1 tbs parsley, chopped finely
Kosher salt
Freshly ground pepper

RINSE CHICKEN and pat dry. Season with salt and pepper. In a bowl, combine garlic, sea salt, ¼ cup olive oil, and Tabasco. Rub chicken with mixture, cover, and refrigerate for 1 hour.

MAKE THE MARINADE: In a large, shallow bowl, combine lemon juice, orange juice, orange zest, remaining olive oil, lemon liqueur, and barbecue sauce. Season to taste with salt and pepper. Add olives, tomatoes, and parsley.

COOK CHICKEN on a preheated barbecue for 20–25 minutes, depending on the thickness, turning occasionally. Remove chicken and baste thoroughly with the marinade.

Lime Chicken
with Mint

2½ lb chicken breast and/or
    thigh fillets
⅓ cup fresh-squeezed lime juice
¼ cup white wine
1–2 chile peppers, seeds removed
    and cut into fine strips
¼ cup green onions, chopped finely
2 tbs mint leaves, chopped finely
½ tsp cumin
Zest from 1 lime
3–4 tbs peanut oil
½ tsp brown sugar
1 lime, cut into 8 segments
2 oz vermicelli noodles
Kosher salt
Freshly ground pepper

RINSE CHICKEN and pat dry. Place in a bowl and season with salt and ground pepper.

IN A SHALLOW BOWL, combine lime juice and white wine. Add chile peppers, onions, mint, cumin, and lime zest. Baste chicken and marinate for 2 hours, turning occasionally.

IN A PAN, heat oil and brown chicken on all sides. Reduce heat and cook 15–20 minutes, turning occasionally. Add marinade and sugar and simmer for 1–2 minutes. Add lime and season to taste with salt and pepper.

PULL APART vermicelli and cook according to package directions.

TO SERVE: Divide noodles onto plates, top with chicken, and drizzle with marinade. Garnish with lime wedges and mint.

Chicken with Peaches and Raspberry Sauce

8 small chicken breast fillets
2 tsp floral honey
1 tbs raspberry vinegar
2 tbs plus ½ cup white wine,
    separated

Raspberry sauce
2 tbs shallots, peeled and
    chopped finely
½ cup fresh raspberries
3¼ cups chicken stock, separated
2 tbs vegetable oil
3 tbs butter, separated

1 cup long-grain rice
Zest from 1 lime
Juice from ½ lime
2 peaches, pits removed and
    cut into wedges
A little powdered sugar
Kosher salt

RINSE CHICKEN and pat dry. Season with salt and pepper and arrange on a plate. Combine honey, vinegar, and 2 tablespoons of wine. Drizzle over the chicken, cover, and marinate in the refrigerator for 20 minutes.

IN A SAUCEPAN, combine shallots and remaining wine and reduce to about ¼ cup. Add raspberries and ¾ cup chicken stock. Reduce by half. In a blender, purée raspberry sauce until smooth and then put through a fine strainer. Season to taste with salt and pepper and set aside.

IN A PAN, heat oil and 2 tablespoons of butter and fry chicken over moderate heat for 10–12 minutes, turning occasionally. Remove from pan and keep warm. Combine pan juices and ½ cup stock, briefly bring to a boil, and add to raspberry sauce.

RINSE RICE under cold water. Combine 2 cups stock, lime zest and lime juice, and bring to a boil. Add rice, season to taste with salt and pepper, cover, and simmer for about 20 minutes.

IN A PAN, melt remaining butter. Add peaches, dust lightly with powdered sugar, and sauté for 1 minute on each side.

TO SERVE: Divide rice on to plates. Arrange chicken and peaches on the top. Drizzle with raspberry sauce.

Chicken, Asparagus, and Strawberry Salad

2 chicken breast fillets
1 tbs olive oil
1 lb asparagus
½ cup strawberries, rinsed
    and sliced
1 cup pineapple, sliced into
    small pieces

Dressing
3 tbs crème fraîche
3 tbs heavy cream
1 heaping tbs ketchup
Pinch of cayenne pepper
Pinch of sugar
1 tsp cognac

2 heads Bibb lettuce
Kosher salt
Freshly ground pepper

RINSE CHICKEN BREASTS and pat dry. Season with salt and pepper. Heat a pan and add oil. Add chicken and cook for 8 minutes on each side. Remove from pan and dice.

FILL POT WITH WATER and steam asparagus until cooked, but firm. Cut asparagus into 1 inch pieces on the diagonal.

IN A BOWL, combine chicken, asparagus, strawberries, and pineapple. Gently mix together.

MAKE THE DRESSING: Whisk together crème fraîche, heavy cream, ketchup, cayenne, sugar, and cognac. Season to taste with salt and pepper.

LINE 4 BOWLS with 2–3 lettuce leaves and top with chicken. Serve dressing in a separate bowl or drizzle over the salad.

Chicken with Spiced Pineapple

2½ lb chicken breast and thigh fillets

Marinade

6 cloves garlic, peeled and
    minced, separated
1 stalk lemon grass,
    chopped coarsely
2½ tsp kosher salt, separated
1 tsp crushed black pepper
2 bay leaves
¼ cup white vinegar
¼ cup light soy sauce

1 fresh pineapple (about 2½ lb)
3 tbs brown sugar, separated
1 tsp turmeric
¼ cup vegetable oil
⅓ cup onions, peeled and
    diced finely
2 star anise
1 cinnamon stick
6 whole cloves
3 tbs fresh ginger root, peeled
    and sliced finely
2 red chile peppers, cut in half
    with seeds removed
Wooden skewers, soaked in water

RINSE CHICKEN, pat dry, and cut into 1½ inch cubes.

FOR THE MARINADE: Combine 4 cloves of garlic, lemon grass, 1½ teaspoons salt, pepper, bay leaves, vinegar, and soy sauce in a bowl. Add chicken, cover, and marinate in the refrigerator for 2–3 hours.

PREPARE THE SPICED PINEAPPLE: Peel pineapple, remove any eyes, and cut into 1 inch pieces. In a saucepan, combine 2 tablespoons of brown sugar and turmeric. Add just enough water to cover pineapple and boil uncovered for 10 minutes. Drain pineapple, setting aside the liquid.

IN A LARGE PAN, heat oil and brown remaining cloves of garlic, onions, star anise, cinnamon stick, and cloves for 2 minutes. Add ginger, ⅓ cup of the set aside pineapple liquid, remaining salt, and remaining sugar. Boil for 2–3 minutes. Add chile peppers and pineapple and simmer for 3–4 minutes.

REMOVE CHICKEN from marinade and thread onto skewers. Place on a preheated grill or under the broiler for 5 minutes on each side, brushing repeatedly with marinade.

TO SERVE: Divide skewers and spiced pineapple onto plates.

Pepper Chicken
with Apricot Jam

⅔ lb chicken breast fillets

1 tbs green peppercorns

1 tbs black peppercorns

2 tbs coarse sea salt

½ cup apricot jam

3 cloves garlic, peeled and
    finely chopped

2 tbs fish sauce (e.g., Vietnamese
    nuoc nam or Thai nam pla)

¼ cup lime juice

Zest from 2 limes

4 oz glass noodles

⅔ cup cucumbers, diced

Fresh mint for garnish

Kosher salt

Freshly ground pepper

Wooden skewers, soaked in water

RINSE CHICKEN and pat dry. Season with salt and pepper, then cut into 1 inch cubes.

IN AN UNGREASED PAN, toast peppercorns until they give off a fragrance (careful not to burn). Cool and crush in a mortar. In a shallow bowl, combine peppercorns, salt, jam, garlic, fish sauce, and lime juice. Stir in zest from 1 lime, add chicken, and cover with marinade. Cover the bowl and place in the refrigerator for 1 hour.

REMOVE CHICKEN from the refrigerator and thread onto skewers. Place on a preheated barbecue and cook over moderate heat for 4–5 minutes on each side. Brush with remaining marinade.

PREPARE GLASS NOODLES according to package directions.

TO SERVE: Sprinkle remaining lime zest over skewers, arrange on plates with glass noodles, and top with diced cucumber. Garnish with mint.

Chili Chicken with Rose Jelly

¼ cup peanut oil, separated
1 red chile pepper, seeds
    removed and cut into
    fine rings, separated
2 tsp fresh ginger root, cut into
    fine strips, separated
1 cup pineapple, cut into chunks
2 cups chicken stock
2 lb assorted skinless chicken pieces
2 tbs rose jelly (found in specialty
    gourmet stores)
Sage leaves
Rose petals
Kosher salt
Freshly ground pepper

IN A PAN, heat 2 tablespoons oil and briefly braise half the chile pepper and half the ginger. Add pineapple and sauté for 3–4 minutes. Remove and keep warm.

IN A SAUCEPAN, reduce stock by half. Rinse chicken and pat dry. Season with salt and pepper. In a pan, heat remaining oil and brown chicken. Add remaining half of chile pepper and remaining ginger. Reduce heat and sauté for 8–10 minutes. Remove chicken, add reduced stock, and bring to a boil. Add jelly and simmer for 5 minutes. Season to taste with salt and pepper. Return chicken to the pan and coat thoroughly with sauce.

TO SERVE: Divide chicken onto plates and surround with pineapple. Drizzle with sauce and garnish with sage leaves and rose petals.

ON THE STOVETOP

THERE ARE PLENTY OF RECIPES for baking chicken in the oven or cooking it on the barbecue, but making a meal on the stovetop is what these are all about. Whether slowly cooking all ingredients in one pot for Chicken with Almonds, or quickly deep-frying Crispy Chicken, this is where the versatile nature of chicken is exposed.

Chicken in
Red Wine

2¾ lb assorted chicken pieces
1 tbs flour
2 tbs butter
3 tbs olive oil
⅔ cup shallots, cut into thin rings
1 cup small mushrooms
2 stalks celery, diced coarsely
1 cup red wine
½ tsp thyme leaves
1 bay leaf
Kosher salt
Freshly ground white pepper

RINSE CHICKEN and pat dry. Rub with salt and pepper and dust the chicken with flour.

IN A LARGE ROASTING PAN, heat butter and oil and brown chicken on all sides. Remove from pan and keep warm. Brown shallots and mushrooms in pan residues until shallots are translucent. Add celery and wine. Return chicken to the pan, and add thyme and bay leaf. Cover and simmer for about 15 minutes.

TO SERVE: Arrange chicken on a deep platter. Remove bay leaf and pour sauce over the top.

Chicken with Almonds

2½ lb assorted chicken pieces
¼ cup vegetable oil
4 celery stalks, sliced
1 bunch green onions,
    sliced into rings
2 carrots, sliced
1 cup hot chicken stock
2 tbs sherry
1 tbs soy sauce
½ cup almonds, sliced and toasted
Kosher salt
Freshly ground pepper

RINSE CHICKEN and pat dry. Season with salt and pepper.

IN A LARGE PAN, heat oil, add chicken, and brown on all sides. Add celery, green onions, and carrots. Cook until they begin to brown. Add ½ cup stock, cover the pan, and simmer over low heat for 40–45 minutes, gradually adding remaining stock. Add sherry and soy sauce. Simmer 5 more minutes.

TO SERVE: Divide chicken onto plates and sprinkle almonds over the top.

Chicken in Spicy Sauce

2½ lb chicken breast and
    thigh fillets
1 tbs fresh ginger root, peeled
    and minced
2 cloves garlic, peeled and minced
⅓ cup onions, chopped
3 tbs light soy sauce, separated
3 tbs dry sherry, separated
¼ cup plus 2 tbs peanut oil
2 chile peppers, seeds removed
    and cut into rings
2⅓ cups chicken stock, separated
1 tbs light rice vinegar
2 tsp brown sugar
2 tbs green onions, sliced into rings
1 tsp ground turmeric
1 cup Thai aromatic rice
Kosher salt
Freshly ground pepper

RINSE CHICKEN and pat dry. Season with salt and pepper. In a large bowl, combine ginger, garlic, onions, 1 tablespoon soy sauce, 1 tablespoon sherry and then add chicken. Baste chicken with marinade, cover, and place in the refrigerator for 30 minutes.

IN A PAN, heat ¼ cup oil. Once oil is hot, add chicken (do not discard marinade) and brown on all sides. Reduce heat and sauté for 15 minutes, stirring occasionally. Add marinade, chile peppers, remaining soy sauce, sherry, 2 cups stock, vinegar, and sugar. Simmer for 5–10 minutes.

FOR THE RICE: Heat remaining oil and braise green onions until translucent. Add turmeric and rice. Pour in remaining stock and bring to a boil. Reduce heat and simmer for 15 minutes, stirring occasionally.

WHEN RICE IS DONE, divide evenly onto plates and arrange the chicken around it. Pour juice over the top.

Yellow Curry Chicken

12 dried red chile peppers

½ cup shallots, peeled and
    chopped coarsely

1 tbs coriander root,
    chopped coarsely

1 stalk lemon grass,
    chopped coarsely

1 tbs cumin

2 tbs turmeric

2¼ lb chicken breast and
    thigh fillets

4 cups coconut milk

⅔ lb small firm potatoes, peeled
    and quartered

1 cup onions, peeled and chopped

⅔ cup carrots, sliced

1 tbs peanut oil

½ tsp salt

2 tbs sugar

¼ cup fish sauce

Mint leaves for garnish

MAKE THE CURRY PASTE: Soak chile peppers in cold water for 20 minutes then drain. In a food processor, combine chile peppers, shallots, coriander, and lemon grass into a smooth paste. Stir in cumin and turmeric. Set aside.

RINSE THE CHICKEN, pat dry, and cut into 2 inch pieces. Season to taste with salt and pepper.

IN A WOK, bring coconut milk to a boil over medium heat and simmer chicken for 10 minutes. Add potatoes, onions, and carrots. In a saucepan, heat oil and add ½ cup of coconut milk from the wok. Stir in set aside curry paste and simmer for 10 minutes. Pour everything back into the wok and season with salt, sugar, and fish sauce. Simmer over low heat for 15–20 minutes. Garnish with mint.

Crispy Chicken

2½ lb assorted chicken pieces
1 red onion, peeled and chopped
3 cloves garlic, minced
3 tbs rum
1 tsp ground oregano
3 tbs chicken stock
Lots of oil or shortening
    for deep-frying
Flour for breading
Kosher salt
Freshly ground pepper

RINSE CHICKEN and pat dry. Season with salt and pepper.

IN A MORTAR OR FOOD PROCESSOR, combine onion, garlic, rum, oregano, and stock. Process into a paste and season with salt and pepper. Rub onto chicken, cover, and refrigerate for at least 6 hours.

IN A DEEP PAN, heat oil or shortening (fat should be about ½ inch deep) to no more than 350°F. If you don't have a thermometer, dip a chopstick into the oil. The oil is hot enough when tiny bubbles form on the chopstick.

DREDGE THE MARINATED CHICKEN in the flour, shake off excess, and slowly fry on all sides until brown and crispy. Drain on paper towels and serve immediately.

Chicken and Lobster

⅓ lb chicken thigh fillets
1 pinch cinnamon
¼ cup butter
1 small onion, peeled and
    chopped finely
4 tomatoes, diced
1 bouquet garni (fresh parsley,
    marjoram, and thyme
    tied together)
1 bay leaf
½ cup white wine
1 tbs cognac
1 lb lobster
⅓ cup olive oil
3–5 saffron threads
2 cloves garlic, peeled
2 tbs almonds, toasted
Kosher salt
Freshly ground pepper

RINSE CHICKEN, pat dry, and cut into 2 inch pieces. Season with salt, pepper, and cinnamon.

IN A LARGE SAUCEPAN, heat butter and fry chicken, turning until golden-brown. Add onion, tomatoes, bouquet garni, and bay leaf. Braise for 5-10 minutes. Add wine and cognac and reduce by half. Add enough hot water to cover chicken and braise over low heat for 10 minutes.

IN A POT, cook lobster in boiling water for 5 minutes, remove, and drain well, patting dry with paper towels. Remove lobster from shell and cut into 2 inch pieces.

IN A PAN, heat oil and brown the lobster. As soon as the meat begins to become firm, transfer to the saucepan with the chicken and cook until both become tender (about 10 more minutes).

IN A MORTAR, crush saffron, garlic, and almonds. Thin mixture with a little warm water and add to the saucepan. Season to taste with salt and ground pepper.

One Pot Chicken

3 lb assorted, boneless
    chicken pieces
½ cup carrots, chopped coarsely
½ cup celery, chopped coarsely
½ cup leeks, white parts only,
    chopped coarsely
⅔ cup small white turnips,
    chopped coarsely
1 cup savoy cabbage,
    chopped coarsely
6–8 cups water
1 small yellow onion, peeled
2 whole cloves
1 tsp black peppercorns
1 stalk parsley
1 bay leaf
Kosher salt
Fresh black pepper

RINSE CHICKEN and pat dry. Place chicken, carrots, celery, leeks, turnips, and cabbage into a large pot. Cover completely with water. Bring to a boil. Reduce heat so that water remains just below the boiling point, skimming off foam as it forms. Stud onion with cloves. Add onion, peppercorns, parsley, bay leaf, and season with salt and pepper. Poach the chicken for about 1 hour.

SERVE CHICKEN in bowls with broth and vegetables.

Chicken Soup
with Meatballs

2½ lb assorted chicken fillet pieces
1 carrot, chopped coarsely
1 celery stalk with leaves,
    chopped coarsely
1 leek, chopped coarsely
1 parsnip, chopped coarsely
1 bay leaf
1 tbs peppercorns
1 onion, unpeeled, cut in half
1 tbs coriander seeds

Meatballs
2 slices stale white bread
½ lb ground meat
1 egg yolk
1 bunch cilantro,
    chopped, separated

1 cup green beans
1 cup carrots, sliced
1 cup snow peas
Kosher salt
Freshly ground pepper

RINSE CHICKEN and pat dry. Place in a large pot and cover with 8 cups of water and bring to a boil. Add carrot, celery, leek, parsnip, bay leaf, peppercorns, onion, and coriander. Simmer for 2 hours, occasionally skimming foam off the top. Remove chicken and pour soup through a strainer lined with a cloth. Let soup cool and ladle off the layer of fat that forms at the top.

FOR THE MEATBALLS: Soften bread in water, mix with ground meat, egg yolk, salt, pepper, and half the cilantro. Shape into small meatballs.

SET ASIDE 1 cup of stock for cooking the meatballs and then bring remaining stock to a boil. Add a pinch of salt, green beans, carrots, and snow peas. Simmer for 15 minutes and then add chicken.

IN THE MEANTIME, cook meatballs in the stock that was set aside and add to the soup at the very end.

BEFORE SERVING, sprinkle with remaining chopped cilantro.

Garlic

Chicken Salad

¾ lb chicken breast fillet
⅓ cup olive oil, separated
1 head frisée lettuce
1 romaine heart
½ cucumber, peeled and diced
2 tomatoes, sliced thinly
1 bunch radishes, sliced

Dressing

3–4 garlic cloves, peeled
    and minced
3 tbs balsamic vinegar
1 tbs water

2 hard-boiled eggs, each
    sliced into 8 pieces
Kosher salt
Freshly ground pepper

RINSE CHICKEN, pat dry, and season with salt and pepper. Heat 1 tablespoon oil in a pan and brown chicken on each side, reduce heat to low and cook for 10 minutes. Wrap in foil and set aside.

RINSE FRISÉE AND ROMAINE and tear into pieces. In a large bowl, combine lettuce, cucumber, tomatoes, and radishes.

MAKE THE DRESSING: Combine garlic, balsamic vinegar, water, and whisk in remaining oil. Season to taste with salt and pepper.

TO SERVE: Divide the salad onto 2 plates and arrange chicken on top. Drizzle with salad dressing and garnish with sliced eggs.

Tagliatelle with Chicken and Tomatoes

1 lb chicken breast fillets, cubed
¼ cup olive oil
½ cup onions, chopped
1 clove garlic, minced
1 lb ripe tomatoes, diced
Pinch of sugar
1 small chile pepper, seeds removed
    and diced
12 oz tagliatelle
1 tbs chopped herbs (e.g., thyme,
    oregano, or parsley)
3 tbs black olives, chopped
Freshly grated Parmesan cheese
Kosher salt
Freshly ground pepper

RINSE CHICKEN and season with salt and pepper. In a saucepan, heat olive oil and sauté onions and garlic until translucent. Add chicken, tomatoes, sugar, chile pepper, and season with salt and pepper. Simmer gently, uncovered for 10–12 minutes.

COOK TAGLIATELLE in boiling, salted water until al dente, according to package directions and drain. Add pasta to the saucepan and toss, adding herbs and olives. Sprinkle Parmesan cheese over the top of pasta, if desired.

INDEX